MAY 2017

The Mole
with a Goal

Tracy Kompelien

Consulting Editor, Diane Craig, M.A./Reading Specialist

ABDO
Publishing Company

Published by ABDO Publishing Company, 4940 Viking Drive, Edina, Minnesota 55435.

Printed in the United States.

Credits
Edited by: Pam Price
Curriculum Coordinator: Nancy Tuminelly
Cover and Interior Design and Production: Mighty Media
Photo and Illustration Credits: BananaStock Ltd., Comstock, Corbis Images, Corel, Digital Vision, Eyewire Images, Hemera, Tracy Kompelien

Library of Congress Cataloging-in-Publication Data

Kompelien, Tracy, 1975-
     The mole with a goal / Tracy Kompelien.
       p. cm. -- (Rhyme time)
     ISBN 1-59197-806-8 (hardcover)
     ISBN 1-59197-912-9 (paperback)
     1. English language--Rhyme--Juvenile literature. I. Title. II. Rhyme time (ABDO Publishing Company)

PE1517.K663 2004
428.1'3--dc22
                                                                          2004050794

SandCastle™ books are created by a professional team of educators, reading specialists, and content developers around five essential components that include phonemic awareness, phonics, vocabulary, text comprehension, and fluency. All books are written, reviewed, and leveled for guided reading, early intervention reading, and Accelerated Reader® programs and designed for use in shared, guided, and independent reading and writing activities to support a balanced approach to literacy instruction.

Let Us Know

After reading the book, SandCastle would like you to tell us your stories about reading. What is your favorite page? Was there something hard that you needed help with? Share the ups and downs of learning to read. We want to hear from you! To get posted on the ABDO Publishing Company Web site, send us e-mail at:

sandcastle@abdopub.com

SandCastle Level: Fluent

Words that rhyme do not have to be spelled the same. These words rhyme with each other:

bowl

mole

coal

pole

foal

roll

goal

toll

hole

whole

Danny dug a tunnel in the snow.

He crawls through the **hole**.

Jordan is eating a **bowl** of cereal for breakfast.

The **mole** peeks out of its burrow.

Wendy's snowman has eyes made out of coal.

Janet is fishing with her parents.
She helps her dad hold the
fishing **pole**.

A baby horse is called a foal.

Nancy likes to lie on her skateboard and roll.

Ryan, Phillip, and Justin are happy because they scored a goal.

Doug has a big hot dog.

He is going to eat the whole thing.

Mr. Vance gives a receipt to everyone who pays the **toll**.

The Mole with a Goal

Molly the mole
had a great goal.

Her goal was to ride
Freddy the foal.

In order to reach her goal,
Molly the mole
had to climb out of her hole.

She had to run past
a large, round fishbowl.

Next she walked to the mud hole,
where she was to pick up a pole.

At the mud hole,
there was a frog on patrol.

He asked for a small toll
for use of the pole.

poles
5¢
each

Once Molly paid the toll,
she took a stroll
to see her friend Freddy the foal.

Freddy the foal
said, "Climb the pole,
but be careful not to let it roll!"

Molly the mole
climbed the pole
and was ready to ride
on the back of the foal.

She was happy
that she reached her goal!

Rhyming Riddle

What do you call
a dish used to collect fees?

Toll bowl

Glossary

burrow. a hole or tunnel dug in the ground by a small animal for use as shelter

coal. a dark brown or black material that is formed underground from fossilized plants. It is mined and burned for fuel

mole. a small mammal that digs tunnels and lives underground

patrol. the act of walking around an area to watch over it and keep it safe

stroll. a slow walk taken for pleasure

toll. a fee or tax paid for a privilege or service, such as driving on a highway or crossing a bridge

About SandCastle™

A professional team of educators, reading specialists, and content developers created the SandCastle™ series to support young readers as they develop reading skills and strategies and increase their general knowledge. The SandCastle™ series has four levels that correspond to early literacy development in young children. The levels are provided to help teachers and parents select the appropriate books for young readers.

Emerging Readers
(no flags)

Beginning Readers
(1 flag)

Transitional Readers
(2 flags)

Fluent Readers
(3 flags)

These levels are meant only as a guide. All levels are subject to change.

To see a complete list of SandCastle™ books and other nonfiction titles from ABDO Publishing Company, visit www.abdopub.com or contact us at:
4940 Viking Drive, Edina, Minnesota 55435 • 1-800-800-1312 • fax: 1-952-831-1632